Looking for Amelia

Story by Heather Hammonds

Illustrations by Meredith Thomas

Rigby PM Plus Chapter Books
part of the Rigby PM Program
Sapphire Level

Published by Harcourt Achieve Inc.
10801 N. MoPac Expressway
Building #3
Austin, TX 78759
www.harcourtachieve.com

U.S. edition © 2004 Harcourt Achieve Inc.

First published in 2003 by Thomson Learning Australia
Text © Heather Hammonds 2003
Illustrations © Thomson Learning Australia 2003

10 9 8 7 6 5 4 3 2
07 06 05

Printed and bound in China by 1010 Printing Limited

Looking for Amelia
ISBN 0 75786 933 5

Contents

Chapter One

Moving

Emily stood in the overgrown front yard of her family's new home and shivered as the winter wind blew a scattering of dead leaves around her feet. She looked up at the front of the house. It seemed to glare angrily back at her, the afternoon sunlight reflecting off its small windows.

"Emily!" called her mom from the front porch. "Mrs. Fraser has a present for you."

Emily sighed and walked slowly toward her mom. Mrs. Fraser was the elderly lady who had sold the house to Emily's family. She was moving to the country to live with her son and his wife. Today, Emily, her big brother Rick, and their parents were moving in.

"My daughter's a little sad to be moving," Emily heard her mom whisper to Mrs. Fraser. "She'll get over it when she starts school here and makes some new friends."

No I won't! Emily thought to herself.

It wasn't that she minded changing schools very much — it was the house they were moving to that bothered her. It was old and dark, and the boards creaked when she went upstairs to her bedroom. Rick, who was studying to be an investigative journalist, thought it was great. He already had crazy plans to make a study for himself in the damp, dark cellar.

"This is a beautiful old house with lots of choices," Emily's dad had said to her after they bought the place. "We'll redecorate your room first, Em. Imagine what it will look like with new wallpaper and a colorful rug on the floor!"

But Emily didn't care what her room would look like. She thought the house was spooky and she longed for the modern city apartment they used to live in.

Mrs. Fraser pushed an old wicker doll carriage out of the front door as Emily approached the porch steps.

"Here you are," she said with a smile. "I found this doll and carriage hidden away in a corner of the cellar, many years ago when my husband and I first moved in. They must have belonged to someone who lived here before us and I think they should stay with the house."

Emily didn't really like dolls, but she smiled politely and looked into the carriage.

"Oh!" she gasped. "She's so pretty!"

Lying on a white silk pillow was a delicate china doll. She wore a blue dress, and her long curly hair was tied with two red ribbons. She stared up at Emily with a sad expression on her face.

"After I found the doll, I cleaned her up and made her a new outfit," said Mrs. Fraser. "She doesn't have a name but maybe you'd like to give her one."

Emily carefully lifted the doll out of the carriage. She looked at her old-fashioned painted features and noticed a tiny chip on her cheek, shaped like a teardrop.

Most dolls are boring, but I love this one, Emily thought. *She looks so unhappy; I wonder who she belonged to and what she was called? A doll like this must have had a special name.*

"Thank you very much, Mrs. Fraser," she said. "I promise to take good care of her."

Chapter Two

Homesick

That night after dinner, Emily climbed into bed in her new room and pulled the covers up to her chin. The wind howled around the old house and a scratching sound on the window pane made her jump.

"It's only a tree branch," she whispered to herself. "Nothing to be afraid of."

She looked at the cardboard boxes on the floor that were full of her belongings, and tears filled her eyes. Just then she would have given anything to be back in the apartment.

A knock at her bedroom door made Emily quickly wipe the tears away.

"Come in," she said.

It was Rick.

"Dad says not to unpack your stuff, Em. We're going to move you into the spare room and start working on your bedroom tomorrow morning. It'll look great in no time!"

Emily knew Rick was trying to cheer her up and was grateful to him. He was the best big brother that anyone could have; he taught her how to play football and basketball, and he drove her to her swimming lessons every week. Rick was eight years older than Emily and they almost never disagreed — unlike her friends, who seemed to argue with their brothers and sisters all the time.

"Are you okay?" asked Rick, coming to sit on Emily's bed.

"I don't like this house," said Emily. "It's really spooky — I bet it's haunted."

Rick laughed. "Of course it isn't haunted! You'll love it once you get used to it," he said, picking up the doll from its carriage. "And what about this doll Mrs. Fraser gave you? Isn't she a beauty!"

"She's the nicest thing about this place," sighed Emily. "But who would leave such a beautiful doll in the cellar?"

"Someone silly," replied Rick. "Anyway, she's yours now."

He put the doll back and left the room. Emily snuggled down in her bed and drifted off to sleep, wondering about her new doll.

Chapter Three

A Mystery from the Past

The next day, everyone was up bright and early. Dad and Rick began work on Emily's room while she and her mother unpacked boxes downstairs. The wind had died down and the sun was shining. Emily began to feel a little happier, so she wandered upstairs to her room to see how the redecorating was going. Rick was standing by one wall, holding a little book.

"Look what I found!" he said. "It was inside a hole in the wall, behind the old wallpaper."

Dad took the book from Rick. "It looks like a diary," he said. He carefully opened it and began to read.

December 27th, 1934

We have just had the best holiday ever, and the first in our brand new house. Uncle Bob came for lunch and I received the most wonderful presents – this journal to write in, a jump rope, a book of adventure stories, and best of all, a new doll! She's so pretty, and even has her own carriage. I've named her Amelia.

"Wow," said Rick. "Maybe Amelia is Emily's doll."

"Can I please read the diary?" asked Emily.

"I suppose so," said Dad. "But show it to Mom first."

Emily decided to read the diary herself, before showing it to her mom. After all, Rick had found it in *her* room. She took it outside and sat on the front porch, turning the old, yellowed pages.

December 28th, 1934

Today has been very cold and sunny. I heard Mother tell Father that we should go to the beach for a vacation. She's worried because some children on our street are sick and she's afraid the sickness will spread to Charles and I. Father said we might go next week.

December 29th, 1934

Charles is being SO horrible lately. He keeps trying to take Amelia. He also pokes his tongue out at me and calls me "Eleanor, Schmelanor."

He's such an annoying little brother!

December 30th, 1934

It was very cold again today. I took Amelia in her carriage for an early morning walk around the house. Charles broke his new wooden top. Father says he's a very naughty boy for breaking his new present already. I'll NEVER break Amelia!

15

December 31st, 1934

Last night Charles stole Amelia and hid her. He wouldn't tell me where he'd put her and she's nowhere to be found. This morning I told Mother what he'd done, but she was too busy to listen because Charles has suddenly become ill. He has a fever and cries all the time. The doctor has been called and I'm not allowed in his room.

I wonder what's wrong with him. I want Amelia back!

January 1st, 1935

It's New Year's Day and so far we are having an awful new year. Charles is very sick and cannot move his legs. Mother and Father took him to the hospital this morning, and Uncle Bob is staying with me. Amelia is still missing, but I'm too tired to look for her just now. My head aches and I have a sore throat. I'm afraid to tell, in case I have to go to the hospital, too.

Emily had reached the end of the diary. None of the other pages had been filled in.

"Poor Eleanor," she whispered, feeling sorry for the sick girl who must have only been a little younger than herself. "What was wrong with her?"

Chapter Four

What Happened to Eleanor?

Emily ran inside and showed the diary to her mom, who quickly read it.

"My goodness," said Mom, looking sad. "Those children must have had polio!"

"What's polio?" asked Emily.

"It's a disease that sometimes leaves people unable to walk, or move their arms and legs properly," Mom explained. "Today, most people in this country can't catch it because they were given a vaccine to protect them when they were little. But many years ago, before the vaccine was invented, lots of people caught polio."

"Did people who caught polio die?" Emily asked.

"Sometimes," said Mom. "Often they were left crippled by the disease."

"I wonder what happened to Eleanor?" Emily sighed. "She didn't write in her diary again ..."

Mom gave Emily a hug.

"We've no way of knowing," she replied. "But I think that we can be pretty sure your doll is the 'Amelia' that Eleanor wrote about."

Emily spent the rest of the day thinking about poor Eleanor and her doll. After dinner she went to the spare room where Rick and Dad had put her bed and all her things. She picked up Amelia and sat her on her knee.

"Now I know your name," she whispered. "I wish Eleanor could have found you before she got sick."

"Feeling sad again?" asked Rick, coming into the room. "Mom told me what was in the diary."

Emily nodded.

"What if Eleanor died from polio?" she said with a shiver. "She might be haunting this creepy old house, looking for her doll."

Rick looked sternly at Emily.

"Stop being silly," he said. "Lots of people got polio and didn't die. Eleanor probably recovered, and even if she didn't, she isn't haunting this house!"

"I wish I knew what happened to her," said Emily in a miserable voice.

Rick sat down and put his arm around her.

"I've just had an idea," he said. "Let me practice my journalism skills and try to find out what happened to Eleanor."

"Do you think you can?" asked Emily.

"I'm not promising anything, but I'll try," smiled Rick. "It will be good to learn about the history of this old place, anyway."

The next morning, Emily went with her parents to choose new wallpaper for her bedroom. When they got back, they found Rick sitting at the kitchen table with the phone book in front of him, looking excited.

"Hey Em, I've been on the Internet and made a few phone calls," he said. "I found the name of the first owner of this house; he was Joseph Appleyard, and he sold the place a couple of months after he bought it. I'm betting Joseph Appleyard was Eleanor's father and he sold the house after the kids got sick."

"Eleanor Appleyard," nodded Emily thoughtfully. "It's a nice name."

"All I have to do now is find out the rest of the story," said Rick.

Emily could hardly wait.

★ ★ ★

A whole week went by. It didn't seem as though Rick was getting any closer to solving the mystery of Eleanor. Every time Emily asked him if he'd found out anything new, he shook his head and said, "Be patient, Em. I'm doing my best."

Every night Emily left a light on in the spare room where she was sleeping. Her imagination ran wild when the old wooden house creaked in the cold winter weather. She was sure a ghostly Eleanor would walk through the door at any moment, wanting to claim her lost doll ...

Chapter Five

A Surprise Visitor

Rick and Dad worked hard on Emily's bedroom. One morning, it was finally finished. The new floral wallpaper Emily had chosen looked beautiful, and Mom had found some pretty curtains to match. The polished wooden floor shone in the morning sunlight and a bright woollen rug lay in the middle of it.

"I wonder what Eleanor would think of this room now," Emily said to Rick, as she put Amelia and her carriage underneath the window. "It must have been her bedroom, too, since she hid her diary in here."

"I think she'd like it," replied Rick, with a smile. "In fact, I'm sure she would."

★   ★   ★

Emily spent the afternoon packing her backpack and sorting through her new schoolbooks. The next day was her first day at her new school and she was feeling a little nervous. She hoped her new classmates would be nice.

Suddenly, she heard a knock at the front door.

"Can you get that, Emily?" called Mom.

With a sigh, Emily ran to the door and opened it.

A very old lady stood on the front porch. She looked rather stern at first, but then she smiled at Emily, and her blue eyes twinkled.

"Hello, I'm looking for a doll named Amelia," she said. "I was told you might know where she is."

Emily gasped and took a step backward.

"W... who are you?" she stuttered.

Rick appeared behind the mystery lady, grinning.

"Emily, I'd like you to meet Mrs. Eleanor Thomas. Before she was married her name was Eleanor Appleyard."

"You can call me Eleanor," said the old lady.

"Oh!" exclaimed Emily. "You didn't die!"

Eleanor laughed and shook her head.

"I certainly didn't, and neither did my brother. Rick has told me all about you and I must say, you're a very kind girl to worry about what happened to me!"

"I tracked Eleanor down through government records," said Rick, grinning at Emily. "Luckily, Appleyard isn't a common name around here."

"It's also lucky that most of my family stayed in this area and you were able to find my nieces and nephews," nodded Eleanor.

Rick led Eleanor inside and into the living room. Emily noticed that she walked with a limp and guessed it was from having polio as a child. It was hard for her to believe that this elderly lady was the same little girl who had written in that diary all those years ago.

"I'll get Amelia," said Emily, running upstairs.

Amelia sat contently in her carriage, staring up at Emily. In a way, Emily was sorry to have to give the beautiful doll back to its rightful owner. She carefully wheeled the carriage out into the hallway and down the stairs.

27

"Here she is," Emily said with a lump in her throat, pushing Amelia over to Eleanor.

"Oh!" said the old lady. "She's just as beautiful as I remember her!"

Emily noticed that Eleanor's eyes were bright with tears, and she reached out and patted her arm.

"The lady who lived here before us found her in the cellar. She cleaned her up and made her a new dress."

"So that's where my naughty brother hid her," said Eleanor. "After he got better, he couldn't remember where she was. I got a new doll, but I never forgot Amelia."

Chapter Six

New Friends, Old Memories

"Why did your parents sell this house so soon after you'd moved in?" Emily asked Eleanor.

"Well, my brother and I caught polio, and they sold it to pay for a special treatment to help us recover," she replied. "Do you know what polio is?"

Emily nodded, so Eleanor continued.

"Charles and I were sick for a long time, and after we got better, neither of us could walk correctly. In those days, polio victims were put into big splints and braces to stop them from moving their damaged arms and legs. Then Father heard of this new treatment and he wanted us to try it. It was invented by a lady named Sister Kenny."

"What was so special about Sister Kenny's polio treatment?" asked Emily.

"She took away the splints and braces and used special exercises to help polio victims walk correctly again," explained Eleanor. "Father took us to one of her special hospitals, where we stayed for several weeks. When we left, we were able to walk quite well again."

"Wow," said Emily. "That's amazing!"

Eleanor stayed for a while. Emily found herself liking the older lady more and more as she listened to her tell stories about the old days, when she was young.

"I loved this place," Eleanor sighed. "And I especially loved my bedroom."

"Come and see it now," said Emily, taking Eleanor by the hand. "Dad and Rick just finished redecorating it for me."

Together they slowly climbed the stairs and stepped into Emily's room.

"Oh, it's beautiful," smiled Eleanor, looking around. "There's only one thing missing . . ."

"What's that?" asked Emily.

"Amelia," replied Eleanor. "Amelia belongs here, and I think you should keep her."

"Really?" gasped Emily. "Are you sure?"

Eleanor nodded. "As long as you promise to come and visit me sometimes and bring her with you."

"I will!" said Emily, giving Eleanor a hug.

Soon it was time for Eleanor to leave. Emily stood in the driveway and waved good-bye as Rick drove Eleanor home. A cold gust of wind blew around her and she shivered again, looking up at the house. She remembered how much Eleanor had loved the old house, and suddenly it didn't seem so scary any more. In fact, it seemed quite inviting.

Smiling, Emily hurried back inside to Amelia. *I'm glad we moved here after all*, she thought.